Improving Local Government Performance Through Tax Optimization

Riyanto Wujarso[1], Saprudin[1], Anton Zulkarnain Sianipar[2],
Revan Andhitiyara[1], Arie Martin Parulian Napitupulu[1]

[1]Sekolah Tinggi Ilmu Ekonomi Jayakarta, Indonesia.
[2]Sekolah Tinggi Manajemen Informatika dan Komputer Jayakarta,
Indonesia.

Acknowledgements

The authors would like to express their profound gratitude and heartfelt appreciation to their esteemed colleagues at the Jayakarta College of Economics and the Jayakarta College of Informatics, Computer, and Management. Their unwavering support, cooperation, and encouragement have played an instrumental role in the remarkable achievement of this research.

First and foremost, we extend our deepest thanks to the exceptional faculty members and administrators of the Jayakarta College of Economic and the Jayakarta College of Informatics, Computer, and Management. Their visionary leadership and unwavering commitment to academic excellence have created an environment conducive to research and intellectual growth. We are truly grateful for their constant guidance and unwavering assistance throughout this enriching journey.

Our sincere appreciation also goes to the brilliant minds within the research department who have contributed immensely to the shaping of this research. Their expertise and invaluable insights have elevated our understanding of the subject matter and influenced the trajectory of our investigation. Engaging in thought-provoking discussions, brainstorming sessions, and receiving constructive feedback from them have been pivotal in refining our ideas and methodologies.

Furthermore, we would like to express our deep gratitude to the dedicated research support staff and technical assistants. Their meticulous attention to detail and unwavering commitment to ensuring the accuracy and reliability of our research findings have been indispensable. Their tireless efforts in data collection, analysis, and documentation have been instrumental in the successful completion of this study.

Furthermore, we are grateful to the participants of this study for their invaluable contributions. Their willingness to share their experiences and perspectives has provided us with essential data, enriching the depth and authenticity of our findings. Their active involvement has played a pivotal role in deriving meaningful conclusions and formulating valuable recommendations.

We would also like to acknowledge the exceptional assistance provided by the dedicated librarians and library staff. Their unwavering support in accessing relevant literature and resources has been vital in expanding our knowledge base and conducting a thorough literature review.

The Jayakarta College of Economics and the Jayakarta College of Informatics, Computer, and Management are also acknowledged with our sincere gratitude for their kind financial assistance. Their support of our research efforts, including data collecting, the acquisition of research materials, and conference attendance, has been crucial to the accomplishment of our study.

And also we would like to give our family, friends, and other loved ones a sincere thank you. They have been a continual source of inspiration and motivation for me during this study journey because of their everlasting support, encouragement, and understanding.

Finally, we would like to express our gratitude once more to everyone who helped this research be completed successfully. Our respected colleagues, academics, research support personnel, participants, and loved ones' unwavering support, collaboration, and encouragement have been crucial to achieving our study goals. We are incredibly appreciative of everyone's knowledge and effort in shaping this study.

Contents

ABSTRACT

Taxes play a vital role in the proper functioning of a country, particularly when it comes to executing various development initiatives. Just as taxes imposed at the federal level impact the overall performance of the government, regional taxes hold equal significance in the operations of state and local authorities. These regional taxes serve a wide range of purposes, including regulation, budget allocation, redistribution of resources, and a combination of these objectives. The effectiveness of a local tax system depends on its ability to generate sufficient revenue, thereby improving the overall functioning of local governments. Consequently, this paper delves into discussions surrounding strategies to optimize local tax collection methods, which aim to enhance the performance of local governments. In this investigation, a descriptive qualitative approach is employed to gain comprehensive insights into the subject matter.

The study findings shed light on the critical requirement of a funding source, primarily sourced from local revenue, referred to as PAD (Own-Source Revenue), for the successful implementation of autonomy and decentralization. It is evident that local taxes and levies should contribute significantly to PAD funding. However, the current state of affairs reveals a substantial insufficiency, as these local taxes and levies only account for a mere 16% of the total PAD. Consequently, there arises a pressing need to maximize the intensification of local tax collection methods and regional levies to bolster regional income and enhance regional performance, as previously mentioned.

In order to improve regional performance and effectively meet the demands of development initiatives, it becomes imperative to explore various strategies aimed at optimizing local tax collections. By doing so, local governments can tap into a more substantial revenue stream, which, in turn, enables them to enhance their operational capabilities. Moreover, such initiatives contribute to the overall improvement of the governance structure at the regional level.

The implementation of autonomy and decentralization requires a stable and substantial source of funding. In this context, the reliance on PAD as the primary funding source becomes apparent. Local revenue generated through taxes and levies holds immense potential in fulfilling the financial requirements necessary for achieving autonomy and decentralization effectively. However, the current scenario paints a bleak picture, as local taxes and levies fall significantly short of their expected contribution to PAD. This financial inadequacy hampers the progress of regional governments and impedes their ability to effectively address the developmental needs of their respective areas.

To overcome this financial shortfall, it is crucial to devise strategies that aim to maximize the intensification of local tax collection efforts and regional levies. By streamlining and optimizing these revenue streams, regional governments can increase their income and, subsequently, their operational capacity. This, in turn, empowers them to fulfill their responsibilities effectively, allocate resources efficiently, and implement developmental projects that cater to the specific needs of their regions.

The optimization of local tax collection methods and the intensification of regional levies not only have a direct impact on regional income but also contribute to the overall improvement of regional performance. By enhancing the revenue streams at the local level, governments can invest in various development initiatives, improve public infrastructure, and provide better public services to the local communities. Moreover, a robust financial foundation enables governments to address socioeconomic disparities, foster economic growth, and promote overall well-being within their regions.

Finally, taxes play a crucial part in the running of a country, and regional taxes are similarly important for state and municipal administrations. Yet, the existing inadequacy of local tax collections and regional levies makes the implementation of autonomy and decentralization difficult. To solve this issue, it is critical to prioritize refining local tax collecting procedures and strengthening regional levies, since these actions have the potential to significantly raise regional income and performance. Governments can efficiently satisfy the needs of development projects, enhance public services, and promote general socioeconomic progress within their regions if they do so.

I. Introduction

Regional taxes play a significant role in the development of the regional economy and the overall progress of a nation. Development at the regional level is a crucial component of national development as it aims to enhance the standard of living and well-being of individuals residing in a specific region. While economic development is often the primary focus, it is important to acknowledge that national or regional development encompasses more than just economic growth. A broader definition of development takes into account various factors and outcomes that contribute to the overall progress of a region (Simanjuntak, 2009).

Economic development is a fundamental aspect of regional growth as it drives the rate of economic growth, which, in turn, stimulates development in other sectors. By achieving fair and inclusive development, opportunities for active participation in the development process are increased, thereby promoting a sense of ownership and empowerment among the residents (Nurani, 2011). To ensure an efficient and successful development plan, it is crucial to pursue development in a harmonious and integrated manner, both within sectors and between regions. This approach aims to achieve regional independence and equitable progress, considering the unique potential and diversity of each region (Rochdianingrum & Setyabudi, 2019).

The key objective in regional development is to achieve regional autonomy by devolving authoritative power to the regions. This decentralization of power emphasizes democratic values such as community participation, equity, justice, and the recognition of regional potential and diversity (Ristanti & Handoyo, 2017). By granting greater authority to regions in managing their own affairs, the government aims to bring services closer to the community, facilitate monitoring and control of regional budget and revenue, and foster healthy competition, inter-regional relations, and the generation of innovative ideas (Namlis, 2018).

A primary goal of implementing regional autonomy is to increase Regional Original Income (PAD), which signifies regional independence in financial management. The Law Number 33 of 2004 defines local revenue as income originating from the regions themselves, and it categorizes the sources of local revenue as regional tax revenues, regional levies, regionally-owned companies, regional wealth management results, and other legitimate local revenue (Nurhayati, 2008). PAD, as a significant contributor to the region's overall income, forms the foundation for local governments' development finance efforts. It enables a greater number of development initiatives and facilitates the faster achievement of community welfare (Prawoto, 2006).

Efforts to explore and maximize local revenue sources, particularly PAD, can be time-consuming due to the need for regular updates to reflect changes in the socio-economic environment, legal requirements, and the demands of the local community for improved government performance (Hertanto & Sriyana, 2011). To optimize PAD results, a state-of-the-art approach is employed, serving as a guide and reference for various systematic processes. Achieving a significant increase in Regional Original Revenue is often accompanied by an increase in regional tax revenues, regional levies, and other legitimate sources of PAD, contributing significantly to the overall growth of regional income.

Other legal sources of PAD include interest on funds deposited in the regional treasury, the impact of the local currency exchange rate, the sale of regional assets, and commissions or deductions from procurement, all of which tend to increase with the growth of the region's economy. Regionally-owned companies and regional wealth management are also additional sources of local revenue (Nurhayati, 2008).

Although local taxes contribute modestly to overall local revenue generation, exploring the possibility of increasing local taxes is crucial for the financial stability and development of local governments. Taxes on hotels, restaurants, entertainment, advertising, and other local activities can provide additional revenue streams that support regional development efforts.

Regional taxes play a similar role to central taxes, contributing to the implementation of state or government functions in terms of regulation, revenue generation, redistribution, and resource allocation (Aji, 2010).

These taxes have two major categories of functions:

1. Budgetary functions.
    Tax budgetary activities are largely concerned with allocating funds for local services. When taxes are paid, they add to the government's overall revenue, which is subsequently distributed to different community-benefiting programs and sectors. Public services including healthcare, education, infrastructure improvement, and social welfare programs are all funded in large part by these levies. Tax revenue allows local governments to support community needs and demands, assuring the delivery of basic services and raising standard of living generally.

2. Regulatory functions.

   Taxes also perform regulatory duties by attempting to keep the process under control. Governments can control economic activity, guarantee adherence to fiscal objectives, and impose financial discipline through the levy and collection of taxes. Governments may influence and shape economic behavior, promote some activities while discouraging others, and address social issues through tax policies. Governments use taxes as a tool to enact laws that advance justice, equity, and social welfare. It aids in wealth redistribution, lowering income disparities, and fostering economic stability.

   By exercising regulatory functions, governments can influence the behavior of individuals, businesses, and other entities. Tax policies and regulations can be designed to incentivize desirable actions, such as investment in certain sectors or the adoption of environmentally friendly practices. Conversely, taxes can also be used as deterrents to discourage undesirable behavior, such as excessive consumption of certain goods or engaging in activities that harm public health or the environment.

Generally, the fiscal and regulatory purposes of taxes promote the effective operation of municipal governments. Tax money helps governments to provide public services and satisfy community needs, while the regulatory component assures adherence to budgetary rules and encourages responsible economic conduct. By optimizing revenue collection, improving resource allocation, and fostering an environment that supports sustainable growth, local governments may boost their financial performance through tax optimization.

1.1 Literature Review

Adi, P. H. (2006), "The relationship between regional economic growth, development spending, and local revenue"

This publication examines the relationship between regional economic growth, development expenditure, and regional own revenue in the context of local governments in Java-Bali. The study finds that changes in expenditure structure significantly impact both regional economic growth and regional own revenue. It suggests that allocating more capital expenditure to support economic growth infrastructures can increase regional own revenue. The publication emphasizes the importance of fiscal decentralization in enabling regions to manage their fiscal capacities and enhance economic efficiency. The research findings align with previous studies that highlight the positive relationship between infrastructure spending and economic growth.

There are several restrictions to take into account, despite the fact that this publication offers insightful information about the connection between spending structure, economic expansion, and regional income. First off, the study's exclusive emphasis on Java-Bali local governments restricts the applicability of its results to other Indonesian provinces. To have a deeper grasp of the subject, it would be advantageous to broaden the sample to include areas outside of Java-Bali.

The article also stresses the necessity of placing a high priority on the standard of public services in order to achieve balanced growth. It does not, however, go into detail about any ideas or tactics for doing this. The influence of quality public service improvements on regional economic development and tax income might be explored in more detail.

Moreover, the study contends that raising regional development spending can boost local tax income and economic growth. While this is a reasonable statement, it would be beneficial to investigate how development spending should be best distributed across various sectors to optimize its effect on income and economic growth. Policymakers may benefit from knowing which industries contribute the most to income and economic expansion.

Overall, this article offers a basis for comprehending the connection between regional own revenue, spending structure, and economic growth. To overcome the aforementioned constraints and offer more detailed advice to policymakers to improve regional economic growth and revenue production, more research is necessary.

Aji, T. S. (2010), "Alternative Models for Building Local Tax and Regional Retribution Planning Information Systems"

The goal of this study is to create and enhance the regional revenue and retribution (PDRD) planning model for the Gresik Regency. The study highlights macroeconomic factors that affect the possibility for parking tax and retaliation (PDRD) for various types of automobiles. A model combining the signal method and probability approach is suggested to forecast the rise of PDRD after the financial capacity of Gresik Municipality has been evaluated. Moreover, the research assesses PDRD's management abilities and pinpoints any problems.

The planning strategy for regional revenue and retribution in Gresik Regency is usefully illuminated by this research, in general. Effective macroeconomic factors that affect PDRD for various vehicle kinds are identified by the study, which also examines the possibility of parking taxes and penalties. An innovative method of forecasting the rise of PDRD is the presented model that combines the signal approach and probability approach.

The situation could be made even better in a few places, though. First, the study might have gone into more depth about the precise macroeconomic factors that were discovered and how they affected PDRD. The knowledge of the elements affecting income creation would have been improved as a result.

Even though the research assesses Gresik Municipality's financial capacity, it would have been advantageous to give specific suggestions or approaches to deal with the problems that were found. The research would have been better served by offering workable methods for enhancing financial planning and management.

Also, the research may have gone further into the possible problems noted in the assessment of PDRD's managerial capacity. It would have benefited policymakers and local government representatives to investigate the sources of these problems and offer solutions.

This research contributes to the understanding of regional revenue and retribution planning in Gresik Regency. It provides valuable insights into the factors influencing PDRD and proposes a novel model for predicting revenue growth. However, further improvements could be made in terms of providing more detailed information, specific recommendations, and addressing the identified issues in management capability.

Asteria, B. (2015), "Analysis of the influence of regional tax revenues and regional levies on district/municipality regional revenues in Central Java"

This study looks at the effects of local taxes and fees on the initial revenue of local governments in Indonesia's Central Java area between 2008 and 2012. According to the data, municipal taxes and fees have a big impact on local income. The research places a strong emphasis on the significance of comprehending the function of regional taxes and fees in providing funding for local governments.

The link between local taxes, fees, and local government revenue in the Central Java area is generally well understood because of the insights provided by this research. The study uses regression analysis, a powerful statistical technique, to examine how municipal taxes and fees affect revenue. The study's conclusions emphasize the importance of enhancing municipal tax and fee collection in order to raise local income.

However, there are a few limitations to consider. Firstly, the research only focuses on the Central Java region, which may limit the generalizability of the findings to other regions in Indonesia. It would be beneficial to conduct similar studies in different regions to obtain a more comprehensive understanding of the impact of local taxes and fees on local government revenue.

The research does not delve into the specific strategies or approaches that local governments can employ to improve the collection of local taxes and fees. Providing practical recommendations or case studies of successful implementation would enhance the practical applicability of the research findings

The research does not explore the potential challenges or barriers faced by local governments in collecting local taxes and fees. Understanding these obstacles would provide a more nuanced understanding of the factors influencing revenue generation.

As a result, although this study adds to our understanding of how local taxes and fees affect local government income in the Central Java region, more study is required to broaden the scope and offer actionable suggestions for enhancing revenue collection.

Ering, S., Hakim, D. B., & Juanda, B. (2016), "Analysis of Regional Tax Potential for Increasing District and City Fiscal Capacity in North Sulawesi"

This research examines the impact of local taxes and fees on the original revenue of local governments in the Central Java region of Indonesia from 2008 to 2012. The findings indicate that local taxes and fees have a significant influence on local revenue. The study emphasizes the importance of understanding the role of local taxes and fees in generating revenue for local governments.

The link between local taxes, fees, and local government revenue in the Central Java area is clarified by this study in useful ways. The study uses regression analysis, a powerful statistical technique, to examine how municipal taxes and fees affect revenue. The study's conclusions emphasize the importance of enhancing municipal tax and fee collection in order to raise local income.

There are some restrictions to take into account. First off, because the study solely considers Central Java, its conclusions could not be applicable to other parts of Indonesia. To have a better knowledge of how local taxes and fees affect local government revenue, it would be advantageous to carry out comparable research in several locations.

The report also doesn't go into detail on the precise methods or tactics that local governments might use to increase the collection of local taxes and fees. The practical application of the study's conclusions would be improved by offering concrete suggestions or case studies of successful implementation.

Also, the study makes no attempt to examine the difficulties or obstructions that local governments could have when trying to collect local taxes and fees. An in-depth study of these challenges would help to clarify the variables affecting income growth. Although this study adds to our understanding of how local taxes and fees affect local government income in the Central Java region, more study is required to broaden the scope and offer actionable suggestions for enhancing revenue collection.

Khatimah, H. (2017), "Sukuk and Their Contribution in Development Financing"

This article looks at how North Sulawesi, Indonesia, might improve its fiscal capability by implementing local taxes. Despite double-digit growth since 2005, the region's tax-to-GDP ratio has stayed constant at about 0.24%. According to the study, local tax potential is significantly influenced by variables including per capita GDP, the agricultural industry, and the number of high school pupils. The quantity of personnel, however, makes little difference. In order to improve the region's fiscal capability and lessen its reliance on payments from the federal government, the study contends that local taxes can be an important factor.

Overall, this article provides valuable insights into the potential of local taxes in North Sulawesi. The study effectively analyzes various factors that influence tax potential and highlights the importance of improving tax effort and efficiency for sustainable development. However, there are a few limitations to consider.

Firstly, the article does not delve into the specific reasons behind the stagnant tax-to-GDP ratio in North Sulawesi. It would have been beneficial to explore potential barriers or challenges that hinder the optimization of tax collection in the region.

Secondly, while the study identifies factors such as per capita GDP and the agriculture sector as significant influencers of local tax potential, it does not provide a comprehensive analysis of their individual contributions. Further research could delve deeper into the specific mechanisms through which these factors impact tax revenue.

Lastly, the article briefly mentions the impact of tax revenue on regional development and local government funding but does not provide a detailed analysis of this relationship. It would have been valuable to explore the extent to which increased tax revenue can contribute to improved public services and infrastructure in the region.

Despite these limitations, this article contributes to the understanding of local tax potential in North Sulawesi and emphasizes the need for effective tax policies to enhance fiscal capacity and reduce dependence on central government transfers. Further research can build upon these findings to provide more comprehensive insights into the determinants and implications of tax revenue in developing countries.

Rochdianingrum, W. A., & Setyabudi, T. G. (2019), "The Linkage Between The Number Of Umkm And The Level Of Technology To Economic Growth In East Java"

This article examines the relationship between the number of micro, small, and medium enterprises (MSMEs) and the level of technology used on economic growth in East Java Province. The study finds that there is a significant relationship between the number of MSMEs and the level of technology used in the economic growth of East Java Province. The higher the number of MSMEs and the level of technology used, the higher the economic growth. The study also highlights the importance of innovation and government support in promoting the growth of MSMEs and their contribution to the economy.

Overall, this paper offers insightful information about how MSMEs, technology, and economic development interact in the province of East Java. Regression analysis is used in the study to analyze how MSMEs and technology affect economic growth, and the results indicate a substantial link. It would have been advantageous to provide more precise information regarding the technique and data sources, though. The paper also adds that earlier studies in the city of Batu had produced opposing results, but it makes no attempt to explain or analyze why. This discrepancy's further investigation would have given the study more substance.

Although the essay stresses the need for governmental assistance for MSMEs, it does not offer any concrete suggestions or policy implications for decision-makers. It would have been more actionable for the paper to include concrete recommendations for government involvement. Overall, this page helps readers comprehend how MSMEs, technology, and economic growth are related, but further study and analysis are required to properly examine the subject.

II. Method

"Improving Local Government Performance Through Tax Optimization," adopts a descriptive qualitative research technique. This approach aims to systematically explain and evaluate the facts and issues related to the topic of study (Moloeng, 2014). The primary objective of this study is to examine the influence of municipal taxes on enhancing regional financial performance. To achieve a comprehensive understanding of the subject matter, a holistic approach is employed.

Qualitative research methods are particularly suitable for closely observing and evaluating specific cases or instances. By thoroughly examining various variables identified by the researchers, valuable insights and conclusions can be drawn from the study (Somantri, 2005).

The descriptive qualitative research technique used in this book's research provides a detailed exploration and analysis of the relationship between municipal taxes and local government performance. By employing qualitative methods, the researchers can delve into the complexities and nuances of the subject matter, capturing the rich context and diverse perspectives surrounding the topic.

To develop a thorough knowledge of the influence of municipal taxes on regional financial performance, the study method entails collecting data from a variety of sources, including :

- Interviews
  By interviewing important participants in the administration of local government, taxation, and financial management, the researchers are able to acquire insightful opinions and viewpoints. The researchers can go deeper into the topic, examine particular concerns, and acquire first-hand data regarding how municipal taxes affect local financial performance through structured or semi-structured interviews. Among others, the interviews may involve community leaders, local business owners, tax specialists, and government representatives.

- Focus groups
  Organizing focus groups provides an opportunity for in-depth discussions among a selected group of individuals who have knowledge or experience related to the study's topic. These group discussions allow the researchers to explore different viewpoints, uncover common themes, and gain a deeper understanding of the collective perceptions and experiences regarding the influence of municipal taxes on regional financial performance. The participants in focus groups may include taxpayers, local government officials, economists, and representatives from relevant organizations.

- Observations
  Through direct observations, the researchers can gather valuable information about the practical implementation of tax policies and their impact on regional financial performance. They may observe the tax collection process, the utilization of tax revenue, and the overall effectiveness of tax optimization

strategies in improving local government performance. Observations can provide real-time insights into the dynamics and challenges faced by local governments in managing their finances through the optimization of municipal taxes.

- Document analysis.
  Analyzing relevant documents such as financial reports, tax regulations, policy documents, and previous studies is crucial for obtaining a comprehensive understanding of the subject matter. By critically examining these documents, the researchers can identify patterns, trends, and key factors that influence regional financial performance through tax optimization. Document analysis helps in verifying and triangulating the data collected from other sources, providing a solid foundation for drawing meaningful conclusions and making informed recommendations.

By employing these various data collection methods, the researchers ensure a comprehensive and multi-faceted exploration of the influence of municipal taxes on regional financial performance. The combination of interviews, focus groups, observations, and document analysis allows for a more nuanced understanding of the subject matter, enabling the researchers to provide valuable insights and recommendations for improving local government performance through tax optimization.

By the use of these qualitative data gathering techniques, relevant stakeholders, such as local government officials, taxpayers, and subject matter experts, may be thoroughly explored in terms of their experiences, views, and opinions.

The researchers also want to take into account all the many aspects and elements that affect how municipal taxes and local government performance are related by using a holistic approach. This strategy makes sure that the research looks at both the larger socio-economic and governmental factors that affect regional growth as a whole as well as the immediate financial effects of tax optimization.

Throughout the research process, the researchers analyze and interpret the collected data, identifying recurring themes, patterns, and trends. They employ rigorous qualitative analysis techniques to derive meaningful insights and draw conclusions that shed light on the effectiveness of tax optimization in improving local government performance.

Also, the study looks at doable suggestions and tactics for policymakers and local government authorities to improve the use of municipal taxes as a way to improve regional financial performance. These suggestions are supported by the knowledge and understanding gained from the qualitative research procedure.

The study described in this book used a descriptive qualitative research approach to examine the impact of local taxes on enhancing regional financial performance. The study seeks to give a thorough grasp of the topic, providing insightful analysis and practical advice for practitioners and policymakers in local government by using a holistic approach and a variety of qualitative research techniques.

In this study, the following methodologies are used in line with the data analysis strategies proposed by Miles, Huberman, and Saldana (2014):

1. **Data Reduction**: The data collected during the fieldwork is a crucial component of the research process. It provides the foundation for analysis and drawing meaningful conclusions. However, raw data can be overwhelming and challenging to navigate. Therefore, data reduction is a vital step in the research methodology used in this book.

   Data reduction involves organizing and structuring the collected data in a systematic manner. The first step is to review the data and identify key variables and categories that are relevant to the research objectives. These predetermined criteria serve as the basis for categorizing the data and creating a framework for analysis.

   Once the variables and categories have been determined, the data is organized and presented in tables. Each table represents a specific aspect of the research, and the data is arranged in a clear and concise manner. This tabular format allows for easier comprehension and comparison of the data points. Categorizing the data based on predetermined criteria provides a structure that simplifies the analysis process. It enables researchers to identify patterns, trends, and relationships within the data more effectively. By condensing the data into organized tables, researchers can focus on the essential information that is most relevant to their research questions.

   The process of data reduction serves multiple purposes. Firstly, it helps in managing the vast amount of data collected during the fieldwork. By condensing and organizing the data, researchers can navigate through it more efficiently and avoid getting overwhelmed. Secondly, data reduction facilitates the identification of key insights and trends within the data. By categorizing and structuring the data, patterns and relationships become more apparent, allowing for a deeper understanding of the research topic.

Moreover, data reduction is an ongoing process that happens throughout the study. When fresh data is gathered or new insights are discovered, the researchers regularly update and adjust the classification and structure of the data. This iterative process ensures that the data is up to date, correct, and relevant to the research objectives.

Finally, data reduction is a key element in the research methodology presented in this book. By structuring and presenting the gathered data in tables based on predetermined criteria, researchers simplify the data for future investigation. This method supports data management, discovering key insights, and promoting a better understanding of the research problem.

2 **Data Display**: Following the process of data reduction, the authors proceed to present the organized data in a visually accessible format, typically through the use of tables. This stage involves a meticulous analysis and interpretation of the information derived from these tables.

Once the data has been condensed and organized into relevant categories, the authors employ various analytical techniques to delve deeper into the collected information. By presenting the data in tables, the authors facilitate a clearer representation of the patterns, trends, and relationships that emerge from the analysis.

The authors invest considerable effort into scrutinizing the data presented in the tables. They carefully examine the content, seeking meaningful insights and connections among the variables under investigation. This meticulous analysis allows them to discern relevant patterns and draw accurate conclusions based on the evidence at hand.

The authors also provide an interpretation of the results obtained during the data presentation phase. They attempt to elucidate the underlying meanings of the data and go beyond simple observations. They are able to distill the information's meaning through this interpretative process, discover important connections that help create a thorough grasp of the study issue, and uncover any probable causative linkages.

And also, offer the data in tables after distilling and classifying the gathered data into informative categories. This visual representation makes it easier to analyze and evaluate the data in depth, allowing the writers to find trends, make judgments, and offer insightful comments about the study topic.

3. **Conclusions/Verification**: The main objective of this investigation is to unearth previously unreported fresh facts and ideas. By analyzing the data gathered, the findings of this study will enhance the body of existing information and offer practical suggestions for enhancing local governments' efficiency through tax optimization.

The researcher's conclusions will help us comprehend how effective tax optimization strategies may improve the operation of local governments. These findings will clarify the role that taxes play in the financial success of local governments and highlight the necessity of achieving financial balance in order to produce positive outcomes.

Also, the findings of this study will provide policymakers, government representatives, and other pertinent stakeholders with useful implications and recommendations. They will receive insightful advice on how to put policies in place to increase revenue from local taxes, regional levies, and balancing funds. These suggestions can help local governments operate more efficiently and effectively overall, which will benefit the communities they serve.

By exploring the intricate relationship between taxation and local government performance, this research endeavors to bridge the gap in existing knowledge and contribute to the advancement of the field. The conclusions drawn from the data analysis will serve as a stepping stone for future research, inviting further exploration and investigation into the realm of municipal taxation and its impact on government performance. The conclusive outcomes and verification obtained from this study will generate new perspectives and insights, enrich the existing body of knowledge, and provide actionable recommendations for improving local government performance through tax optimization.

By adopting a descriptive qualitative research method and employing data reduction, data display, and conclusion/verification techniques, this study aims to provide a comprehensive understanding of the relationship between local taxes and regional financial performance. The findings of this research will contribute to new knowledge in the field and offer practical recommendations for enhancing the performance of local governments through tax optimization.

III. Result And Discussion

1. Taxes as Local Revenue (PAD)

The government aims to stimulate economic growth, and both the federal and local governments play a crucial role in achieving this objective. At the regional level, economic development focuses on promoting local economic expansion and increasing Regional Original Income (PAD) (Mahi, 2005).

To implement the Regional Budget (APBD) and foster development that enhances community welfare, each local government must establish a reliable PAD. Therefore, it is essential for both the federal and local governments to augment regional budgets. Local taxes emerge as a potential revenue source for the region. The collection of local taxes must adhere to the relevant tax collection laws, which are regularly revised to align with societal changes (Novalita, 2007)

Public services that are not directly funded by people, such as infrastructure, education, and healthcare, are financed by taxes. Tax collection can be enforced as necessary. Taxes, according to Rochmat Soemitro (1990), are sums of money that people pay into the state coffers in accordance with enforced rules, without anticipating any immediate in-kind benefits.

These payments can be verified and used to directly pay for public expenses. Similar to this, R. Santoso Brotodihardjo (2013) defines taxes as sums of money that citizens contribute to the state's coffers in accordance with valid laws, but without directly observable exchanges of goods or services (contra-achievements). To pay for daily costs, taxes thus imply a transfer of wealth from the people to the government coffers. Any excess is countered by public savings, which are the main source of funding for public investments.

Taxes can be perceived in various ways. Simply put, taxes are funds used by the government to improve the lives of citizens. Taxes also contribute significantly to the people's economy. From a legal perspective, taxes fall under state finances, necessitating government regulations to govern state finances. Financially, taxes are considered an essential component of state revenues. Sociologically, taxes are seen from the community's perspective, involving the effect and impact on society regarding costs and outcomes that can be conveyed to the community itself (Suyanto & Pratama, 2018).

To overcome the financial constraints faced by many regions, several measures have been implemented, such as the enactment of Regional Regulations (Perda) that impose taxes and fees to increase Regional Original Income (PAD). The ability of regions to exercise autonomy in managing their finances is influenced by various variables. The primary variables include: financial, organizational, and community capabilities, which form the core foundation for regional autonomy. These variables are further supported by geographical and sociocultural factors, which provide additional context, and political and legal aspects, which add unique dimensions to the equation (Adi, 2006).

One of the main goals of fiscal decentralization is to create regional autonomy. In this perspective, local governments (pemda) are expected to explore local financial resources, particularly through Local Own-Source Revenue (Sidik, 2002). The dependence on transfers from the central government from year to year should be increasingly limited. Oates (1995) provides rational reasons why local governments should reduce this dependence:

Central transfers are usually accompanied by certain conditions, compromising relative autonomy, especially when transfer funds are the dominant source of local revenue. Dependence on transfers actually reduces local creativity in making policies related to more efficient local revenue collection (Adi, 2006).

PAD, or Regional Original Income, is a crucial concept in the realm of regional finance and governance. It encompasses the various sources of income that a region generates through the collection of funds, which are then utilized to finance routine expenses and support the implementation of government policies and regional development initiatives. In other words, PAD represents the ordinary income that is derived from the efforts of the regional government to maximize the utilization of regional financial resources.

The concept of PAD highlights the importance of financial self-sufficiency for regional governments. By generating their own income, regions can reduce their dependence on transfers and grants from the central government. This financial independence is a key objective of fiscal decentralization, as it allows regions to exercise greater autonomy and decision-making power in managing their own affairs.

The sources of PAD can vary from region to region, but they generally include regional taxes and levies, which are considered conventional revenue sources. These taxes and levies are imposed on various economic activities and transactions within the region, such as property taxes, sales taxes, and business licensing fees. By collecting these revenues, regions are able to finance their day-to-day operations, invest in infrastructure development, and provide public services to their residents.

The significance of PAD goes beyond its monetary value. It also serves as an indicator of a region's financial capacity and performance. A higher PAD reflects a region's ability to effectively mobilize and manage its financial resources, indicating a stronger regional economy and governance. It demonstrates the region's capability to generate revenue internally and reduces its reliance on external funding.

Efforts to optimize PAD often involve adopting strategies to enhance revenue collection and broaden the tax base. This can include implementing efficient tax administration systems, improving taxpayer compliance, and exploring new revenue sources. By maximizing PAD, regions can strengthen their financial position, increase their fiscal resilience, and expand their capacity to meet the needs and aspirations of their communities.

Achieving a robust and sustainable PAD requires a comprehensive approach. It involves not only increasing revenue generation but also ensuring the efficient and effective utilization of these funds. Regions must strive for transparency and accountability in managing their financial resources, allocating them towards priority areas and projects that contribute to regional development and public welfare.

The concept of PAD emphasizes the need for regions to align their fiscal policies and practices with national economic objectives. While regions aim to achieve financial independence, they must also adhere to national regulations and fiscal frameworks to maintain fiscal discipline and macroeconomic stability. Collaboration between regional and central authorities is essential to strike a balance between regional autonomy and national cohesion.

PAD plays a vital role in the functioning of regional governments and their pursuit of fiscal decentralization. It represents the income generated by regions through the collection of various funding sources and serves as a measure of their financial self-sufficiency. By optimizing PAD, regions can strengthen their autonomy, enhance their financial capacity, and promote sustainable regional development (Saraswati, 2019)

According to Khatimah, 2017, the collection of regional taxes and levies plays a significant role in contributing to regional income and supporting the financial operations of regional governments. These taxes and levies are fundamental financial instruments utilized by many countries to generate revenue at the regional level. They serve as a reliable and sustainable source of income that enables regional governments to finance a wide range of initiatives, including urban infrastructure development and the provision of essential public services commonly known as "public goods."

Regional Tax Revenue serves three primary purposes, each essential for the effective functioning of regional governments. Firstly, it finances current investments through a pay-as-you-go approach. This means that the revenue generated from regional taxes and levies is allocated to support ongoing projects and initiatives that aim to enhance the quality of life and well-being of the region's residents. These investments could include the construction of roads, bridges, schools, healthcare facilities, and other infrastructure projects that are crucial for the region's development.

Secondly, regional tax revenue is utilized for servicing debt payments. Regional governments often borrow funds to finance major projects or cover budget deficits. The revenue generated from taxes and levies is allocated to meet these debt obligations, ensuring that the region maintains a healthy financial position and remains capable of accessing credit markets for future funding needs. This responsible debt management allows regional governments to sustain their operations and maintain fiscal stability.

Lastly, setting aside funds for future investments is another critical purpose of regional tax revenue. Regions need to plan and prepare for future development projects, which require financial resources. By allocating a portion of the revenue towards a reserve or investment fund, regional governments can accumulate funds over time and strategically utilize them for future investments that align with the region's long-term goals and aspirations. This proactive approach ensures that the region remains well-prepared for future needs and opportunities, promoting sustainable development and economic growth.

The efficient and effective collection of regional taxes and levies is essential for maximizing the revenue potential and achieving financial autonomy at the regional level. Regional governments need to implement robust tax administration systems, enforce compliance with tax regulations, and employ modern technologies to streamline the collection process. This ensures that taxpayers meet their obligations and that the revenue collection is conducted in a transparent and accountable manner.

Moreover, regional governments should continuously evaluate their tax policies and identify opportunities to broaden the tax base. By exploring potential areas for expanding the tax system, such as introducing new tax categories or revising tax rates, regions can enhance their revenue generation capacity. However, it is crucial to strike a balance between increasing revenue and maintaining a conducive business environment, as excessive tax burdens may hinder economic growth and discourage investment.

Regional taxes and levies constitute a vital component of regional income and play a crucial role in financing various aspects of regional development. The revenue generated from these taxes supports current investments, debt payments, and future projects, ensuring the sustainable growth and well-being of the region. By implementing efficient tax administration systems, promoting compliance, and exploring opportunities for broadening the tax base, regional governments can enhance their revenue generation capacity and achieve greater financial independence.

By implementing regional taxes and levies, local governments can mobilize additional financial resources to support their development agendas. These resources are instrumental in meeting the increasing demands for public services and infrastructure improvements within the region. Furthermore, the revenue generated from regional taxes plays a vital role in ensuring the financial sustainability of the region, enabling it to address immediate needs while also planning for long-term investments and contingencies.

The utilization of regional taxes and levies requires careful consideration and strategic planning. Local governments need to strike a balance between maximizing revenue generation and maintaining a conducive business environment to promote economic growth. It is essential to design tax systems that are fair, transparent, and efficient to ensure compliance and minimize tax evasion. Moreover, the revenue collected should be allocated effectively and efficiently, prioritizing key sectors and addressing the specific needs of the local community.

In summary, regional development and financial autonomy are closely linked, with Regional Original Income (PAD) playing a crucial role in supporting regional growth and development. By implementing regional taxes and levies, local governments can increase their revenue streams, which are vital for financing public goods, infrastructure development, and meeting the evolving needs of the local community. However, the effective utilization of regional taxes requires careful planning, fair taxation systems, and efficient allocation of resources to ensure sustainable and equitable regional development.

Regional taxes consist of various financial instruments, including specific taxes and levies that are mandated by law. These taxes play a crucial role in financing urban infrastructure development and the provision of public services, which are commonly referred to as "public goods."

At the regional level, various tax types are designated to contribute to the revenue of the region. These taxes are specifically imposed and regulated by the law to ensure a consistent and structured collection process. Here are some examples of designated taxes commonly found at the regional level :

1. Motor Vehicle Taxes
   These taxes are imposed on motor vehicles, such as cars, motorcycles, trucks, and other types of vehicles. The tax amount is usually based on the type, engine capacity, and value of the vehicle. Motor vehicle taxes are an important source of revenue for the region, as they generate income from vehicle owners within the jurisdiction.

2. Surface Water Taxes

   Surface water taxes are levies imposed on activities related to the use, extraction, or utilization of surface water resources within the region. This tax is commonly applied to industries, agriculture, and commercial activities that rely on surface water sources for their operations. The revenue generated from surface water taxes can be used to support environmental conservation efforts or water resource management projects in the region.

3. Cigarette Taxes

   Cigarette taxes are specific taxes imposed on the sale and consumption of cigarettes within the region. These taxes aim to discourage smoking, promote public health, and generate revenue for the region. The tax rate is typically based on the quantity or value of cigarettes sold, and it can vary depending on the region's regulations. The revenue generated from cigarette taxes can be used for healthcare programs, public awareness campaigns, or other initiatives related to tobacco control.

It is important to note that the availability and applicability of these designated tax types may vary between regions or countries. Some regions may have additional specific taxes or levies based on their unique circumstances or local needs. The implementation and management of these designated taxes require proper administration and enforcement to ensure compliance and maximize revenue collection. Designated taxes play a crucial role in the financial sustainability of regional governments. They provide a diversified revenue stream that can support various development projects, public services, and infrastructure improvements in the region. Additionally, these taxes can be adjusted or modified based on the region's economic conditions, priorities, and policy objectives.

The collection of designated taxes such as motor vehicle taxes, surface water taxes, and cigarette taxes contributes significantly to the revenue generation at the regional level. By effectively managing and optimizing these tax types, local governments can enhance their financial capacity and improve their ability to meet the needs and aspirations of their communities.

However, the collection of designated taxes may vary depending on the circumstances and tax potential of each province. In certain cases, a province may not collect all the designated taxes if the tax potential in a particular area is considered insufficient. This means that the types of taxes collected can differ between regions.

For instance, in regions that are not divided into regencies or cities, such as the Special Capital City Region of Jakarta, the tax collection may involve a combination of provincial and regency/city taxes.

When it comes to regency or city taxes, the range of categories expands even further. These categories include :
→ Hotel Tax
→ Restaurant Tax
→ Entertainment Tax
→ Advertising Tax
→ Street Lighting Tax
→ Non-Metal and Rock Mineral Tax
→ Parking Tax, Groundwater Tax
→ Nest Tax for Swallows
→ Rural and Urban Land and Building Taxes
→ Land and Building Rights Acquisition Fees

It is crucial to remember that the tax potential of a regency or metropolitan region may have an impact on how certain sorts of taxes are collected. Certain specific tax kinds may not be collected in that location if the tax potential is judged insufficient.

Regional taxes include a range of authorized tax forms and levies. These taxes are essential for funding the construction of urban infrastructure and the delivery of public services. Although certain tax types apply at the regional level, others may differ based on the tax potential and administrative divisions within the area. Regency or municipal taxes are diversely collected and include a variety of areas, but their application may also be impacted.

2. Optimization of Tax Collections to Increase Regional Finances as an Effort to Improve Regional Government Performance.

The ability of an autonomous territory to raise its own money is the most important indicator of its ability to govern itself. These autonomous areas must be able to explore their financial resources, manage and utilize them to finance the administration of their regional governments. To ensure that Regional Original Income (PAD), particularly local taxes and levies, remains the major revenue source for the state government, it must be kept as independent from central assistance as possible. This is a precondition for the state government system as a whole (Sumarmi, 2010).

In order to boost regional financial capability, it is vital to maximize PAD sources. As a result, the subject and object of income must be bolstered and expanded. In the short term, the most practical action is to increase the value of existing assets or sources of regional revenue, particularly through the use of information technology. It will be possible to boost PAD's output without having to introduce additional sources or objects of regional income that would necessitate extensive research and time-consuming procedures (Horota et al., 2017).

Because the current tax collection system is less than ideal, it is important to create an integrated information technology support system in order to increase tax collection. The customary collection techniques and procedures reflect this issue, and many of these systems are still partially operational. This means that the information communicated is likely to be incoherent, with many copies of the data and outdated information. It's difficult to collect taxes due to a lack of information on taxpayers and their contributions, as well as a lack of tax invoices and ideal tax compliance targets.

In the short term, the most convenient and expeditious approach to augment regional income is to assess its potential and compile an information database to capture that potential. Enhancing the effectiveness and efficiency of existing regional income sources and objects, rather than expanding them, is the key to boosting productivity in regional revenues. Expanding sources or objects of net income would necessitate extensive research, lengthy procedures, and a significant amount of time. By constructing a database that incorporates variables representing each revenue category, it becomes possible to estimate the revenue generated.

These actions lay the groundwork for establishing "proper" regional revenues and serve as the responsibility of local governments, but only in the medium term. Initiatives to increase regional revenues must be carried out with precision to avoid eroding the public's trust in the government and the Regional Representative Council (DPRD). Unfocused and short-term increases in regional income, benefiting only select groups, can undermine trust. Therefore, the DPRD can optimize the growth of regional revenues by accurately determining the potential of each type of regional revenue (through potential database preparation) and implementing systems and procedures for revenue collection that align with the local community's situation and conditions.

When it comes to increasing regional income, there are a number of methods the Regional Government can use to do so, including optimizing the intensity of collection of regional taxes and regional levies, among others:

- Increasing the source of income New and potential taxpayers, as well as the number of taxpayers, have been identified as potential sources of revenue for the regions, as have object databases, assessments, and projections of revenue capacity for each type of levy.

- Increasing the efficiency of the collection process. Efforts have been made to bolster the collection process, including expediting the development of regional regulations, modifying tariffs, most notably retribution rates, and expanding human resources. Strengthen monitoring This can be accomplished, among other things, by conducting spontaneous and periodic inspections, streamlining the supervisory process, imposing punishments on tax arrears and tax authorities, and increasing tax payments and services supplied by regions.

- Efficiencies in administration and cost savings in collection. The regions' actions include streamlining tax administration procedures and increasing the efficiency of each sort of collection.

- By improving planning, you can increase revenue capacity. This can be accomplished by enhancing coordination with regionally relevant agencies.

Furthermore, tax extensification can also be carried out through government policies to provide further taxation authority to regions in the future. For this reason, it is necessary to change the Indonesian tax system itself through a direct distribution system or several tax bases of the central government that are more appropriately collected by the regions.

An idea has emerged among experts, scholars, and practitioners in fiscal decentralization to grant local governments the power to levy taxes. This can be observed from the analysis of consolidated revenues of the Regional Budget (APBD) and the National Budget (APBN), which includes revenues from regencies/cities, provinces, and domestic sources in the APBN. The share of Regional Original Income (PAD) in the total consolidated revenues is only 5.30%, while expenditures that fall under the responsibility of the regions account for approximately 30% of consolidated expenditures. This illustration of PAD's portion in total consolidated revenues highlights the centralized nature of revenue allocation between regencies/cities and provinces, and domestic revenue in the state budget.

In comparison, developing countries, transition countries, and OECD countries have an average share of 9.27%, 16.59%, and 19.13% of PAD to total consolidated revenues, respectively. This situation hampers the accountability of regional budgets, as regions ideally should be able to cover their limited funding from the central government by adjusting the tax base or regional tax rates. Therefore, there is a need to explore measures to enhance regional taxing power, including the complete transfer of certain central taxes to regions (allowing regions to fully determine the tax base, rates, and collection administration), the allocation of a portion of non-tax state revenue (PNBP) to regions, and other related policies. Regencies and cities should be granted additional income by empowering them with the authority to collect taxes up to a certain extent. Property Tax (PBB) and Acquisition of Rights over Land and Buildings Tax (BPHTB) can be converted into regional taxes.

Regency and city governments have the discretion to determine the tax base and rates for these two types of taxes, with a predetermined cap. In the meantime, the central government will continue to oversee certain aspects.

The Personal Income Tax (PPh) Articles 21 and 25/Article 29, which are currently decentralized to the regions, can be transferred in either an open or piggyback manner, provided that the regions are granted the capacity to impose open transfers up to a specific maximum, with full support from the regency/city governments. Furthermore, it is expected that this regulation would discourage regional initiatives to explore PAD sources that have a negative economic impact.

On the other hand, regarding the authority that falls under the responsibility of the regions, Indonesia is considered a country that has implemented decentralization through a "big-bang" process. This can be observed from the shift in the regions' expenditure assignment, which increased from 16.59% of the Total Consolidated Expenditure (APBD+APBN) in the 1990s to 27.78% in 2021.

IV. CONCLUSION

The effective implementation of regional autonomy heavily relies on the availability of suitable funding sources. The economic potential of a region plays a vital role in enhancing its financial capacity for local governance. However, in the context of the Unitary State of the Republic of Indonesia, regional autonomy is not solely determined by the amount of Regional Original Income (PAD) achieved but also by the region's ability to utilize taxes as a means to regulate the local economy, foster growth, and ultimately improve the welfare of the region and its residents.

Regional taxes, as a component of regional revenue, should serve as the principal source of income for the region. This shift towards greater financial independence from the central government is crucial for the region's autonomy. By relying more on its own revenue sources, the region becomes less dependent on central government transfers and gains greater control over its financial resources. This increased fiscal autonomy allows the region to make independent decisions regarding resource allocation and prioritize its development initiatives according to local needs and aspirations.

However, it is important to approach the procurement of new taxes with caution, considering the current social, economic, and political conditions. Introducing new taxes should be done carefully to avoid causing turmoil within the community, which could have adverse effects on the region's economic activities. Any tax implementation should be thoroughly assessed to ensure its fairness, effectiveness, and economic feasibility. Additionally, it is crucial to ensure that the tax aligns with the local context and is well-suited to the region's specific circumstances.

When considering the establishment of a new tax, it is essential to take into account both the general criteria applicable to taxes and the suitability of the tax as a local tax. While general tax criteria such as equity, simplicity, and efficiency should be considered, the focus should also be on how the tax can contribute to the improvement of public services. A well-designed and properly implemented local tax can generate revenue streams that can be allocated to enhance public services, infrastructure development, education, healthcare, and other essential areas. By improving the quality and availability of public services, the economic performance of the region can be positively influenced, attracting investments, promoting business growth, and enhancing the overall well-being of the local community.

The introduction of a new tax should be accompanied by a comprehensive communication and education strategy to ensure that the rationale behind the tax is effectively communicated to the public. This includes providing clear information about the purpose of the tax, how the revenue will be utilized, and the benefits it will bring to the region. Transparency and accountability in the tax collection and utilization processes are essential to maintain the trust and support of the community.

In summary, the realization of regional autonomy requires the presence of adequate funding sources. The economic potential of a region is instrumental in enhancing its financial capacity for local governance. While regional autonomy is not solely measured by the amount of PAD achieved, regional taxes should be the primary source of revenue for the region.

However, caution should be exercised when introducing new taxes to avoid social and economic disruptions. It is essential to carefully evaluate the suitability of a tax as a local tax and consider its potential to improve public services and the region's economic performance. By striking a balance between regional tax autonomy and responsible tax implementation, regions can achieve greater financial independence and effectively promote their own development agendas.

REFERENCES

Adi, P. H. (2006). "Hubungan antara pertumbuhan ekonomi daerah, belanja pembangunan, dan pendapatan asli daerah." Simposium Nasional Akuntansi IX, 23-26.

Aji, T. S. (2010). "Model Alternatif untuk Membangun Sistem Informasi Perencanaan Pajak Daerah dan Retribusi Daerah." Jurnal Ekonomi Pembangunan: Kajian Masalah Ekonomi dan Pembangunan, 11(2), 160-171.

Asteria, B. (2015). "Analisis pengaruh penerimaan pajak daerah dan retribusi daerah terhadap pendapatan asli daerah kabupaten/Kota Di Jawa Tengah." Jurnal Riset Manajemen Sekolah Tinggi Ilmu Ekonomi Widya Wiwaha Program Magister Manajemen, 2(1), 51-61.

Brotodihardjo, R. S. (2013). "Pengantar ilmu hukum pajak." Bandung: Refika Aditama.

Ering, S., Hakim, D. B., & Juanda, B. (2016). "Analisis Potensi Pajak Daerah untuk Peningkatan Kapasitas Fiskal Kabupaten dan Kota di Sulawesi Utara." Jurnal Ekonomi dan Pembangunan Indonesia, 17(1), 75-87.

Fretes, P. N. D. (2017). "Pengaruh dana perimbangan, pendapatan asli daerah, dan pertumbuhan ekonomi terhadap indeks pembangunan manusia di Kabupaten Kepulauan Yapen." Jurnal Akuntansi & Ekonomi FE. UN PGRI Kediri, 2(2), 1-33.

Hertanto, I., & Sriyana, J. (2011). "Sumber Pendapatan Asli Daerah Kabupaten dan Kota." Jurnal Ekonomi & Studi Pembangunan, 12(1), 76-89.

Horota, P., Riani, I. A. P., & Marbun, R. M. (2017). "Peningkatan Pendapatan Asli Daerah dalam rangka Otonomi Daerah melalui potensi pajak dan retribusi daerah di Kabupaten Jayapura." Jurnal Kajian Ekonomi Dan Keuangan Daerah, 2(1).

Khatimah, H. (2017). "Sukuk Dan Kontribusinya Dalam Pembiayaan Pembangunan." Optimal: Jurnal Ekonomi dan Kewirausahaan, 11(1), 83-103.

Lutfi, A. (2006). "Penyempurnaan Administrasi Pajak Daerah dan retribusi Daerah: Suatu upaya dalam optimalisasi penerimaan PAD." Jurnal Ilmu Administrasi dan Organisasi: Bisnis & Birokrasi, 14(1), 1-9.

Mahi, R. (2005). "Peran Pendapatan Asli Daerah di Era Otonomi." Jurnal Ekonomi dan Pembangunan Indonesia, 6(1), 39-49.

Miles, H., & Huberman, A. M. (2016). "Saldana. (2014). Qualitative

Data Analysis. A Methods Sourcebooks, Edition, 3."

Moloeng, L. J. (2014). "Metode Penelitian Kualitatif." Bandung: Remaja Rosdakarya.

Mulyanto, D. (2002). "Potensi Pajak dan Retribusi Daerah di Kawasan Subosuka Wonosraten Provinsi Jawa Tengah." Jurnal Akuntansi Sektor Publik.

Namlis, A. (2018). "Dinamika Implementasi Penyelenggaraan Pemerintahan Daerah." Jurnal Kajian Pemerintah: Journal Of Government, Social And Politics, 4(1).

Novalita, B. S. (2007). "Peranan pajak daerah dalam meningkatkan pendapatan asli daerah kabupaten Bogor." Universitas Gunadarma.

Nurani, N. (2011). "Efektivitas Sistem Hukum Perbankan Syariah dalam UU N0 21 Tahun 2008 dan Dampaknya pada Pembangunan Ekonomi." Jurnal Ekonomi dan Keuangan Islam, 1(2), 207-216.

Nurhayati, N. (2015). "Analisis Potensi Pajak Daerah Dalam Meningkatkan Pendapatan Asli Daerah Kabupaten Rokan Hulu." Cano Ekonomos, 4(2), 97-108.

Nurhayati, S. (2008). "Pendekatan QSPM Sebagai Dasar Perumusan Strategi Peningkatan Pendapatan Asli Daerah Kabupaten Batang, Jawa Tengah." Jurnal Ekonomi Pembangunan: Kajian Masalah Ekonomi dan Pembangunan, 9(1), 72-82.

OECD (2019): "Taxing Powers of State and Local Government." OECD Publication Service, France.

Prawoto, N. (2006). "Analisis Elastisitas Dan Tingkat Kesulitan Realisasi Penerimaan Sumber Keuangan Daerah Di Kabupaten Sleman." Jurnal Ekonomi & Studi Pembangunan, 7(1), 15-34.

Ristanti, Y. D., & Handoyo, E. (2017). "Undang-undang otonomi daerah dan pembangunan ekonomi daerah." Jurnal RAK (Riset Akuntansi Keuangan), 2(1), 115-122.

Rochdianingrum, W. A., & Setyabudi, T. G. (2019). "Keterkaitan Antara Jumlah Umkm Dan Tingkat Teknologi Terhadap Pertumbuhan Ekonomi Di Jawa Timur." EKUITAS (Jurnal Ekonomi dan Keuangan), 3(4), 543-562.

Saraswati, D. (2019). "Pengaruh Pendapatan Asli Daerah, Ukuran Pemerintah Daerah, Leverage, Terhadap Kinerja Keuangan Pemerintah Daerah." Jurnal Akuntansi Bisnis dan Publik, 9(2), 110-120.

Sidik, M. (2002). "Optimalisasi pajak daerah dan retribusi daerah dalam rangka meningkatkan kemampuan keuangan daerah." Makalah disampaikan Acara Orasi Ilmiah. Bandung, 10.

Simanjutak, T. H. (2009). "Kepatuhan Pajak (Tax Compliance) Dan Bagi Hasil Pajak Dalam Perekonomian Di Jawa Timur." Jurnal Ekonomi dan Studi Pembangunan (Journal of Economics and Development Studies), 1(2).

Soemitro, R. (1990). "Asas dan dasar perpajakan." Bandung: Eresco.

Somantri, G. R. (2005). "Memahami metode kualitatif." Makara Human Behavior Studies in Asia, 9(2), 57-65.

Sumarmi, S. (2010). "Pengaruh Pendapatan Asli Daerah, Dana Alokasi Umum, dan Dana Alokasi Khusus Terhadap Alokasi Belanja Modal Daerah Kabupaten/Kota di Provinsi DI Yogyakarta." Jurnal. Fakultas Ekonomi Universitas PGRI Yogyakarta.

Suyanto, S., & Pratama, Y. H. (2018). "Kepatuhan wajib pajak orang pribadi: Studi aspek pengetahuan, kesadaran, kualitas layanan dan kebijakan sunset policy." Jurnal Ekonomi Dan Bisnis, 21(1), 139-158.

Todaro, M. P. (1995). "Reflections on economic development." Books.

Udjianto, D. W. (2003). "Pendapatan Asli Daerah Dalam Pembiayaan Pengeluaran Rutin Daerah Kabupaten Kulon Progo (1990/91_1999/2000)." Jurnal Ekonomi & Studi Pembangunan, 4(1), 49-63.

Widyaningsih, A. T. (2018). "Pengaruh Pajak Daerah, Retribusi Daerah, dan Produk Domestik Regional Bruto Terhadap Kapasitas Fiskal Kota Pontianak." Jurnal Ekonomi Bisnis dan Kewirausahaan (JEBIK), 7(3), 215-237.

Wujarso, R., Saprudin, S., Sianipar, A. Z., Andhitiyara, R., & Napitupulu, A. M. P. (2022). Improving Local Government Performance Through Tax Optimization. Journal of Governance, 7(1), 110-120.

ABOUT THE AUTHOR

Assoc. Prof. DR (C) Riyanto Wujarso, S.E., Ak., M.M., BKP, is one of the authors of the book "Improving Local Government Performance Through Tax Optimization." He is affiliated with the Sekolah Tinggi Ilmu Ekonomi Jayakarta (Jayakarta College of Economics), Indonesia. With his expertise in economics and taxation, Riyanto Wujarso brings valuable insights to the book's research on enhancing local government performance through tax optimization.

Saprudin, another contributor to the book, has made significant contributions to the study. His expertise and knowledge in the field of taxation have enriched the research on tax optimization and its impact on local government performance. Saprudin's insights and analysis contribute to the comprehensive understanding of the subject matter.

Martin Parulian Napitupulu, as a co-author, has provided valuable inputs and perspectives to the research on improving local government performance through tax optimization. With his background and expertise, Martin Parulian Napitupulu has contributed to the analysis and discussions on the influence of managerial in enhancing regional performance.

Revan Andhitiyara, as a member of the author team, has played a crucial role in the development of the book. With his insights and contributions, Revan Andhitiyara has helped shed light on the holistic approach used to thoroughly examine the influence of financial on regional performance.

Anton Zulkarnain Sianipar, another co-author of the book, is affiliated with the Sekolah Tinggi Manajemen Informatika dan Komputer Jayakarta (Jayakarta School of Informatics, Computer, and Management), Indonesia. With his expertise in informatics management and technology, Anton Zulkarnain Sianipar has provided valuable insights into the role of technology in optimizing tax processes and improving local government performance.

Together, the authors from Sekolah Tinggi Ilmu Ekonomi Jayakarta and Sekolah Tinggi Manajemen Informatika dan Komputer Jayakarta have combined their expertise, research, and insights to produce "Improving Local Government Performance Through Tax Optimization." Their collective knowledge and contributions make this book a valuable resource for understanding the potential impact of tax optimization on local government performance.